BEAUTIFUL AND FAVOURED

ESTHER, THE JEWISH GIRL

BLESSING AJOBA

This book is dedicated to God almighty for the inspiration to write this book.

CONTENTS

CHAPTER ONE
THE BEGINNING

Once upon a time, there lived a girl in the city of Jerusalem named Esther. She was so beautiful and her beauty could melt the heart of everyone one that looked upon her. Esther was smart, obedient and bold, she did whatever her parent asked of her and that made them proud. She was still very young when her parent passed away, so she was taken in by her uncle, Mordecai.

Mordecai was his father's younger brother and he was a godly man. He loved Esther as his own child, he taught her to serve God and rely only on Him.

Before now, there was war between the king Ahasuerus and the king of Jerusalem. King Ahasuerus wanted to reign over all the countries, so he fought them one by one and defeated them including Jerusalem because God helped him.

Jerusalem was a city of God's people but were neglected by God during the battle because they turned their back on God to serve other gods that could not save them. So God allowed their enemy to rule over them. The king took over their lands, riches, cattle, sheep, oxen and donkeys and not only Jerusalem but other countries as well, numbering to one hundred and twenty-seven provinces.

King Ahasuerus ordered his men to bring some of the people as slaves. Mordecai, Esther and his family were among them that was taken as slaves. On getting to the kingdom, some of them were made to be maids, gardeners, gateman and so on. Mordecai was among the people that stayed at the palace gate, he stays there all the time doing his work with joy and gladness not minding his situations.

After the war, in the third year of his reign, king Ahasuerus was celebrating his victory, so he hosted his princes, servants and the nobles in Shushan palace. The palace courtyard was beautifully and elaborately decorated with white and blue cotton curtains tied with linen and purple cords to silver rings on marble columns.

Silver and gold couches were arranged on a mosaic pavement of porphyry, marble, mother-of-pearl, and colored stones. And when the party started, drinks were served in gold chalices, each chalice one-of-a-kind. The royal wine flowed freely. The guests could drink as much as they liked, the king ordered the waiters.

Much wine, much talks. The king talked about his kingdom and showed them his wealth, gold, silver and many more and the party lasted for one hundred and eighty days.

Meanwhile, the Queen by name Vashti was throwing a separate party for the women at another location within the King's royal palace. And with the king's heart was merry with wine, he sent his servants to bring before him Queen Vashti, wearing her royal crown, in order to display her beauty to the people and nobles, for she was very lovely to look at. But when they conveyed the king's order to Queen Vashti, she refused to come.

This made the king very furious and he burned with anger. So the king issued a royal decree and it was written in the laws of Persia and Media, which cannot be repealed, that Vashti is no more the queen and she will never be allowed to enter the presence of King Ahasuerus again.

Later, when King Ahasuerus anger had cooled and the effect of the wine gone, he was thinking over everything that happened during feasting and he remembered what Vashti had done and what he had ordered against her, he regretted his actions but could not do anything to change it.

Questions

1. What is the name of the girl in this story?
2. Who took Esther in?
3. Why did Mordecai, Esther and his family have to leave Jerusalem?
4. Mordecai was made to be ___________ at the palace?
5. Was Mordecai happy with his present situation?

6. Why was queen Vashti banished?
7. Was the King drunk?

Moral Lessons

1. Don't be proud
2. Serve only the living God
3. Don't be a drunkard
4. Always be joyful no matter your experiences
5. When you are smart, obedient and bold you make your parent proud.

CHAPTER TWO

THE GATHERING OF FAIR VIRGINS

It's was a sunny day in Shushan, the weather was really nice and the wind breezed across the city. The birds were singing melodiously, every street was crowded with people and everyone is busy with their businesses. The tables of the moneychangers were full, those selling doves were at their stands and people were all over the place buying and selling. There was a smell of something tasty that makes everyone's mouth watered and lots of people clustered at the place, oh my world! it was a pastry store. You could see everyone trying to buy. Also there were other stands, with different kind of tasty food.

At the palace, lots of king's servants were at the front gate with a scroll in their hands containing the order of the king to all the provinces. The order stated that every province should appoint officers for the king's course. The appointed officers were to gather all the fair and beautiful virgins in the lands and bring them to the king's palace, in the house of the women, unto the custody of Hega the king's chamberlain, the keeper of the women for their purification until the day the king will choose one of them as his wife and will become the queen.

The elections of the officers were done and dusted, followed immediately by the proclamation of the King's edict of careful selection of beautiful damsels in the provinces. Graceful maidens were picked and among them were the daughters of the nobles and commoners.

Esther the adopted daughter of Mordecai by favour was also selected and brought with others to the palace in Shushan. All of them under the care of Hega. Immediately Hega set his eyes on Esther he was pleased with her, not just because of her beauty but also of her elegance and from that moment she won his favour.

Hega provided her with first rated beauty treatments, packed special food for her, assigned to her seven maids selected from the king's palace and placed her and her maids in the best place within the king's harem. On getting to the palace, she looked around in bewilderment and with her mouth wide opened which suggested she has never seen anything as beautiful as that all her life. It was a well-furnished and garnished environment. The wall was painted with white and pink glossy paints which explained the beauty of the shinning and elaborately decorated hall. Also, hanging on the walls were artistic painting of notable events in the history of the state.

The bedroom is another beauty to behold by the eyes. Between the windows were light pink flowered curtains.

At one end was a large family bed with a clean and plain silky bed cover and lying gently upon it were many pillows gorgeously packed in designer pillow case. Within this confine were large two imported pure leather sofa beckoning and begin to be sited upon.

This arrangement made the room cozy was warm. Esther had a look of satisfaction all over her faces and She couldn't have asked for more. But she thought within herself, good things are prepared for those that trust in the Lord and almost everyone could hear her thought as she let out a faint smile.

Hega, the king's chamberlain could not explain why he so much liked Esther and neither could he explained why he treated her differently from others. But from all indications, it was God perfecting everything for Esther and only this conclusion could have explained the kindness and love she received not only from Hega but also from everyone she came in contact with.

Some of the maidens were beautiful and robust while some were skinny and beautiful, some were neither robust nor skinny, yet they were still gorgeous. Esther also was young, about 5'5 feet tall and beautiful with a not too long face and arched nose, also, she had a platinum hair and a pair of beautiful topaz eyes. Born with a milky skin and well curved body.

Since Esther is now within the palace, this gave Mordecai

the effrontery to come within the court from time to time, but most times unnoticed, just to check on Esther. Meanwhile, Mordecai had charged Esther not to disclose their relationship to anyone. He told her to keep it as a secret until the appropriate time.

Hega, the keeper of women had announced to them that their preparation will last for twelve months before appearing before the king in the king's hall. He further explained to them that the first six months is for ministering oil of myrrh and other six months is for sweet odours and other things for purifying for women. All of them were excited at the news, and were like, if it’s like this now, how about when you eventually be crowned the queen? So each one determined to put in their best and do whatever it takes so as to be the chosen one.

Questions

1. The maiden that were gathered would become what?
2. Why was Esther favoured?
3. What is the name of the king chamberlain that was in charge of the maiden?
4. What secret did Mordecai asked Esther not to disclose to anyone?
5. How many months will the maidens stayed before the appearing at the king's hall?
6. What are the purifying items?

Moral Lessons

1. When God likes you, no one can dislike you.
2. It is good to be obedient.
3. Always be kind to people.

CHAPTER THREE

CHOOSING THE QUEEN

Just like the speed of light, the twelve months had gone by. The time everyone anticipated has finally come. Now, each maiden will go to the king's hall in the evening and stay with him till morning and whosoever the king is delighted in and called by name, will be the queen and if rejected, will return to the other house of the women to become one of the king's concubines for life.

Now, when it was Esther's turn to go to the king, she asked for nothing other than what Hega recommended. The items she was given includes Blue Rose Oil which revitalize and makes the skin bloom, with a heavenly scents and was given other scents used for bathing that helps the skin.

After her bath, the maids assigned to her helped her dressed. Did her nails, hair and make-up. Her plain face was beautified, she was stunning and won the admiration and comments from everyone around.

After she was done checking out herself, she was ushered in to the room for her gown and accessories. The gown was beautiful with a sky blue colour. Her jewelries were set of Sapphire and diamond and were magnificently sparkling. All these took much time, as they were at it from morning till evening that one could be tempted to say, it was a waste of time. But it was never a waste of time as none of them is expected to appeared before the king gorgeously and not just anyhow

Then Esther was taken to King Ahasuerus in his private quarter at the royal palace. When she entered, the king stood up to receive her, he was mesmerized by her magnificent beauty. She was heavenly, God clothed her with His glory, she looks radiant and victorious like an angel, He held up his hand towards her which she received gracefully with a smile, she slightly bowed to show her respect. Then she raised her head and her face meet with the king's, she stole his heart in an instant.

Now the king was attracted to Esther more than to any of the other women, and she won his favor and approved her more than any of the other virgins. The king didn't bother to asked about her name but set a royal crown on her head immediately and made her queen instead of Vashti.

Questions

1. What and what did Esther asked for?
2. Who are the people that helped in dressing her?
3. What covered are like a clothes?
4. Who was attracted to Esther?
5. Who was queen instead of Vashti?

Moral lesson

1. Because of pride Vashti lost everything--- so don't be proud.
2. Depend solely on God to work out the best for you.
3. God doesn't leave us when we need him most.
4. God is always behind the scene working for our good.

CHAPTER FOUR

THE FEAST

The king proclaimed a public holiday for a great feast. It was a banquet in Esther's honor and all the princes and servants of the king are expected to be in attendance. For this special occasion, the commercial life in the kingdom was technically shut down, as all roads leads to the palace. All the streets were virtually emptied as everyone found their way into the palace.

It was a very busy day in the palace, people were everywhere. All the palace maids were extremely engaged. The palace wall was looking radiant from the repaint recently done, the flowers were in their blooming season and beautifully pruned.

In the palace hall, chairs and tables were in order and neatly covered with white table covers and decorated with beautiful table flowers neatly arranged in a flower vase. Even the pillars in the hall were beautifully adorned.

It was already mid-day, the event kick started with the king's speech. In his speech, he appreciated everyone present and charged the governors to see to the satisfaction of all the guests. Immediately the king ended his speech, foods and drinks flows freely, everyone ate to satisfaction and some even went home with surplus and heartwarming gifts.

There is joy and happiness in the atmosphere, both the singers and dancers delivered according to as they were paid. By the time darkness descended upon the palace, some were already drunk from excess wine and were in stupor. And with that, conversations could be heard loudly and faintly both from far and near.

But suddenly the party was over and everyone returned to their places. Days went by and everything returned back to normal and activities resumed normal operations.

On a certain day, Mordecai was on duty at the palace, two of the king's eunuchs, Bigthana and Teresh guards at the door of the king's private quarters became angry at King Ahasuerus and plotted to assassinate him. But unknown to them Mordecai eavesdropped and heard every of their plans and quickly ran to Queen Esther to reveal their plans.

Queen Esther immediately told the king about the matter. Ahasuerus the king investigated the matter and the truth was found. Therefore, the king commanded that both of them should be hanged on a tree. Thus Mordecai saved the life of the king that day.

Questions

1. Why was there public holiday?
2. The Feast was in honour of who?
3. Gift were given to everyone by who?
4. ____________and ____________planned to assassinate the king.

Moral Lesson

1. Always keep the right company.
2. Don't disregard information no matter who gave it.
3. Mordecai still retained his job even though Esther is now the queen.

CHAPTER FIVE

HAMAN PLANNED THE DESTRUCTION OF THE JEWS

Sometimes later, King Ahasuerus promoted Haman son of Hammedatha the Agagite to prime minister, making him the most powerful official in the empire next to the king himself. Everyone bowed and reverenced Haman according to the king's commandment. Haman enjoyed every bit of it as he moved about.

But of all the people in the land only Mordecai refused to pay homage to Haman. Other servants noticed this and spoke to Mordecai day after day about a change but he refused still. Finally, Mordecai refusal to honour Haman with a bow was reported to Haman. This got him infuriated and he made up his mind to find out by himself how true their claim. Next day when he got to the king's palace, he purposely looked towards Mordecai's direction and when he saw that Mordecai would not bow down or show him respect, he was practically in rage.

He looked for a way to eliminate Mordecai. Meanwhile, he already discovered that Mordecai was a Jew, so he hated to waste his fury on just him but all Jews throughout the whole kingdom of Ahasuerus.

In the month of April, Haman and his men began to plan and they also cast lots (the lots were called Purim) to determine the best day and month to take action in executing their schemes. And they agreed on March 7 the following year.

Furthermore, Haman approached King Ahasuerus and said, “There is a certain race of people scattered through all the provinces of your empire. Their laws are different from those of any other nations, and they refused to obey even the laws of the king. So it is not in the king's interest to let them live. So If it pleases Your Majesty, issue a decree that they be destroyed, and I will give 375 tons of silver to the government administrators so they can put it into the royal treasury.”

The King laughed and told him to keep his money, but go ahead and do as he like with the people. The king agreed and confirmed his decision by removing his signet ring from his finger and gave it to Haman son of Hammedatha the Agagite the enemy of the Jews.

On April 17 Haman called in the king's secretaries and dictated letters to the princes, the governors of the respective provinces, and the local officials of each province in their own scripts and languages. These letters were signed in the name of King Ahasuerus sealed with his ring. And sent by messengers into all the provinces of the empire.

The letters decreed that all Jews young and old, including women and children must be killed, slaughtered and annihilated on a single day and their properties be given to their killers. This was scheduled to happen exactly on April 17 nearly a year later.

By the king's order, a copy of the document was to be issued as a law in every province, published for all people to read and be ready for that day.

The couriers took the letter and went on their way, the order was also posted in the Shushan palace. The king and Haman sat back talking and had a drink while the city of Shushan were in perplexity from the sad news.

When the news got to Mordecai, he was so furious that he tore his clothes and put on a sackcloth with ashes and went out to the city and cried bitterly, He also went to the palace gate and cried. Also all the Jewish people in Ahasuerus kingdom wept, wailed and wore sackcloth, some even went on fasting. But it was obvious that this tragedy was to befall them because of Mordecai's disobedience to the King's order.

One of the queen's maid and her chamberlain took notice of Mordecai crying at the gate and told queen Esther about it and what has been arranged against the Jews. Then she was exceedingly grieved, she sent her maid to give Mordecai clothes but Mordecai refused it. But gave

Hathach a copy of the decree issued in Shushan that called for the death of all Jews, and he asked Hathach to show it to Esther. He also asked Hathach to explain it to her and to urge her to go to the king to beg for mercy and plead for her people.

The queen sent Hathach to inform Modecai that anyone who tries to appear before the king in his inner court without invitation has signed his death warrant and is doomed to die unless the king holds out his golden scepter.

And explained further that "the king has not called for me in more than a month. But go and gather together all the Jews of Shushan and fast for me. Do not eat or drink for three days, night or day. My maids and I will do the same. And then, though it is against the law, I will go in to see the king. If I must die, then I am willing to die." Mordecai actions also put the life of queen Esther at risk.

So Mordecai went away and did as Esther told him. All the Jews fasted and prayed, even their animal did not eat. By this, they handed over the battle to God and invited God to fight for them.

On the Third day, Esther put on her royal robes and entered the inner court of the palace, the king was sitting on his royal throne, facing the entrance. When he saw Queen Esther standing there in the inner court, he was pleased and welcomed her by holding out the golden scepter to her. So Esther approached and touched its tip and bow slightly.

Then the king asked her, "What do you want? And promised to give you even to the half of my kingdom." So queen Esther knew right there that God had answered their prayers.

Queen Esther answered and said she only requested the presence of the king and Haman in the banquet that she had prepared for him. However, Haman was so happy but restrained himself not to show how happy he felt to be the only one invited with the king, but When he got home he gathered together his friends and Zeresh, his wife, and told them how the queen loved him and had invited only him and the king to her banquet.

Then he added, "But all this is meaningless as long as I see Mordecai the Jew just sitting there at the palace gate. So his wife Zeresh and all his friends said, build a gallow of seventy-five feet high. First thing in the morning speak with the king get him to order Mordecai to be hanged on it. Then after this is done happily go with the king to dinner. So Haman liked the advice and decided to kill Mordecai before the initial set date, and planned to carry it out the following morning.

Questions

1. Who was promoted?
2. Who was not obeying the king's command?

3. Why was Haman furious?
4. How did the Jews planned to fight back?
5. How does queen Esther gain the attention of the king?

Moral Lesson

1. Always obey every law. The disobedience of Mordecai almost cost the whole Jewish people their lives.

CHAPTER SIX

HAMAN PLANNED THE DESTRUCTION OF MORDECAI

It was night, the city became very quiet, the stars brighten the sky and there was a gentle feel of the breeze on the skin. It was a night out, no single person was on the street except for Haman and few of his guard, his heart was full of excitement and his face couldn't hide his happiness. He was on his way to the palace to meet with the king and asked for his permission to hang Mordecai before the morning.

In the palace, king Ahasuerus was on his bed turning like the hinges turns upon the door trying all he could to sleep but couldn't because God deprived him of sleep. So he rose up and called in his guard to bring him the book of the chronicles and read it to him. As he opened to read to him, he came across the place where Mordecai had exposed the plot of Bigthana and Teresh the two royal eunuchs who guarded the entrance but had conspired to assassinate the King.

On hearing this, the king asked, what honor or recognition was given to Mordecai for this? Nothing has been done for him," his attendant answered. While this was going on, at the same time Haman arrived at the king's court. The king ordered his servants to bring in Haman.

When he entered the king's room he bowed to show homage and after their normal pleasantries, the king asked him about what would be appropriate for the man the king specially wants to honor?" Haman in a deep thought, said to himself, "the king must be talking about me or who else could he be?

So he answered the king with joy, the man the king delights to honor, should be clothed with the king's royal robes, and should also drive the king's horse with a royal emblem placed on his head. The king should Instruct one of his most noble princes to dress the man in the king's robe and lead him to the city square on the king's own horse, He continued. The prince is to be commanded to shout as they go, "This is the man the king wishes to honor".

After he got through with his flamboyant rhetoric, the king was pleased and commended him for his excellent counsel but also commanded him to hurry and get the robe and his horse and do just as he has said to Mordecai the Jew, who sits at the gate of the palace. "Do not fail to carry out everything you have suggested" charged the king.

So Haman left the palace with the robe and put it on Mordecai, placed him on the king's horse and led him to the city square, shouting, this is the man the king wishes to honor.

Afterward the parade, Mordecai returned to the palace gate, but Haman hurried home dejected and completely humiliated.

Questions

1. Why was Mordecai honoured?
2. Who honoured him?
3. Why did Haman counsel the king the way he did?
4. Was the King pleased with his counsel?
5. Who did Haman suggested to carry it out?

Moral Lesson

1. Haman is always full of himself.
2. Always have good thought about others.
3. Don't be selfish in thought towards others

CHAPTER SEVEN

QUEEN ESTHER PREPARED A BANQUET FOR THE KING

Queen Esther was busy instructing one of her maids when the king's presence was announced, she rush down to the door and met him and Haman, she bowed in honouring the king, as the manner of the day. She welcomed and led them to sit where they will partake of what was prepared for them and as soon as they were comfortable, she gestured to the maids to serve them.

After they were done eating and while they were drinking wine, the king broke the silence and said, "tell me what you want, Queen Esther. What is your request? I will give it to you, even if it is half of the kingdom." Then Queen Esther replied "Your Majesty" if you are pleased with me and wants to grant my request, then my petition is that my life and the lives of my people should be spared.

For my people and I have been handed to those who would slaughter and annihilate us. If we had only been sold as slaves, I could remain quiet, for that would have been a matter too trivial to warrant disturbing the king.

Then the king was wrath and said who would do such a thing? Who dare lay a hand on my wife and the queen of this land? King Ahasuerus demanded. Who would dare touch you?

Esther said, "The adversary and enemy is this evil Haman." Then Haman was terrified before the king and queen. The king got up in a rage, left his wine and went out into the palace garden and summon some of his guards. But Haman, realized that his end has come because the king had already decided his fate, so he stayed behind to beg Queen Esther for his life. But while he was begging due to the shock he fell on the same sit queen Esther was sitting in a way anyone coming in would think that he wants to molest the queen.

This incident greeted the king when he returned from the garden. To the point that the he roared out, "Will you even molest the queen while I'm just around the corner?" immediately, the blood drained from Haman's face and before he could explain himself, his face was covered by the king's guard.

Then Harbona, one of the king's eunuchs, informed the king, how Haman has set up gallows that stands seventy-five feet tall in his own courtyard, intending to hang Mordecai, the king's saviour. So the king commanded that he should be hanged in the same gallows.

So they hanged Haman, ten of his children and his wife on the gallows he had set up for Mordecai, and the king's anger was pacified. After the execution of Haman and his household, King Ahasuerus gave the estate of Haman, the enemy of the Jews to queen Esther.

Questions

1. What is the motive behind the banquet?
2. Who prepared the banquet and for who?
3. What happened in the banquet?
4. What the mission accomplished?
5. What happened to Haman?

Moral Lesson

1. Always forgive the person who offended you
2. Don't look down on people.

CHAPTER EIGHT

MORDECAI APPOINTED SECOND IN COMMAND!

Now the queen came to the king's quarter to seek an audience with the him. As soon as she sighted the king, she knelt down at his feet with tears flowing freely from her eyes. Again the king held out the golden scepter to Esther. So she rose and stood before him and said, "If Your Majesty is pleased with me and if he thinks it is right, send out a decree reversing Haman's orders to destroy the Jews throughout all the provinces of the king. And having said that, she let the cat out of the bag by telling him her relationship with Mordecai and the king commanded Mordecai to be brought before the king.

The king took off his signet ring which he had taken back from Hamann and gave it to Mordecai and announced him as his second in command.

King Ahasuerus replied Queen Esther and to Mordecai and said, “because Haman attacked the Jews, I have given his estate to Esther and he has been hanged in the gallows. Now write another decree in the king's name in behalf of the Jews as seems best to you, and seal it with the king's signet ring, for no document written in the king's name and sealed with his ring can be revoked."

Mordecai summoned royal secretaries on the 25th day of the six month. And they wrote out all Mordecai's orders to the Jews, and to the princes, governors and nobles of the 127 provinces stretching from India to Cush. These orders were written in the script of each province and the language of each people and also to the Jews in their own script and language.

Mordecai wrote in the name of King Xerxes, sealed the dispatches with the king's signet ring, and sent them by mounted couriers, who rode fast horses especially bred for the king.

Then Mordecai put on the royal robe of blue and white and the great crown of gold, and he wore an outer cloak of fine linen and purple. And the people of Sushan celebrated the new decree.

Mordecai recorded these events and sent letters to the Jews near and far, throughout all the king's provinces, encouraging them to celebrate an annual festival on these two days which was supposed to be the day the whole Jew dies but was turned.

He told them to celebrate these days with feasting and gladness and by giving gifts to each other and to the poor. This would commemorate a time when the Jews gained relief from their enemies, when their sorrow was turned into gladness and their mourning into joy.

Questions

1. who wrote in the king's name?
2. Who made Mordecai the second in command?
3. Do the Jew live happily after they were vindicated?

Moral Lesson

1. Always be kind to people.
2. Always think about your actions so you won't bring problem to those that are closer to you.

ABOUT THE AUTHOR

Blessing Ajoba

is a prolific writter of many children novels. She has a unique gift of translating the Bible stories to suit the daily life of the children.

She enjoys working, teaching and training of children. Her passion for the good upbringing of children is what has lead into writting of many children books.

Blessing is wonderfully married to her husband Ezekiel and they are blessed with three wonderful children.

www.ingramcontent.com/pod-product-compliance
Lightning Source LLC
LaVergne TN
LVHW020535160826
845677LV00015B/4073

* 9 7 9 8 4 1 3 9 5 2 3 2 0 *